STO

FRIENDS
OF ACPL

W9-CZX-132

VELOCIRAPTOR

A Buddy Book
by
Richard M. Gaines

ABDO
Publishing Company

Allen County Public Library
900 Webster Street
PO Box 2270
Fort Wayne, IN 46801-2270

VISIT US AT

www.abdopub.com

Published by ABDO Publishing Company, 4940 Viking Drive, Edina, Minnesota
55435. Copyright © 2001 by Abdo Consulting Group, Inc. International copyrights
reserved in all countries. No part of this book may be reproduced in any form without
written permission from the publisher.

Printed in the United States.

Edited by: Christy DeVillier
Contributing editors: Mike Goecke, Matt Ray
Graphic Design: Denise Esner, Maria Hosley
Cover Art: ©1999-2001 Christopher Srnka, title page
Interior Photos/Illustrations: pages 4, 6, 20, 21 & 27: M. Shiraish ©1999 All rights
reserved; page 14: Bruce E. Shillinglaw; page 15: Denise Esner; page 17: ©Douglas
Henderson from *Living with Dinosaurs* by Patricia Lauber, published by Bradbury
Press; page 18: ©Douglas Henderson from *How Dinosaurs Came to Be* by Patricia
Lauber, published by Simon & Schuster; page 23: Luis V. Rey.

Library of Congress Cataloging-in-Publication Data

Gaines, Richard, 1942-
    Velociraptor/Richard M. Gaines.
        p. cm. – (Dinosaurs)
    Includes index.
    ISBN 1-57765-490-0
    1. Velociraptor—Juvenile literature. [1. Velociraptor. 2. Dinosaurs.] I. Title.

QE862.S3 G39 2001
567.912—dc21

00-069987

TABLE OF CONTENTS

Velociraptor
va-LOSS-ah-RAP-tor

The Velociraptor's name means "quick burglar." Indeed, the Velociraptor was one of the fastest dinosaurs.

The Velociraptor wasn't a huge dinosaur like the Apatosaurus. The Velociraptor was about six feet (two m) long from nose to tail.

It was only about three feet (91 cm) tall. That is taller than a Dalmatian dog.

This meat-eating dinosaur had sharp teeth and claws. It had about 80 teeth. Some of these teeth were over one inch (three cm) long.

The Velociraptor had a large brain. This dinosaur could hear, see, and smell very well.

HOW DID THEY MOVE?

Like a cheetah, the Velociraptor could run very fast. It could probably run about 40 miles (64 km) per hour.

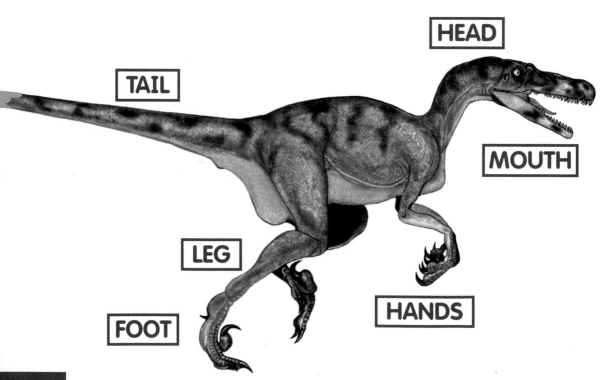

HEAD

TAIL

MOUTH

LEG

HANDS

FOOT

This dinosaur had a lightweight body with long arms and legs. It ran with its two back legs.

The Velociraptor could not run fast for a long time. After about 15 seconds, it had to slow down.

The Velociraptor's prey could not run as fast as the "speedy burglar." Yet, the prey could run for a longer period of time. So, the Velociraptor needed to catch its prey quickly.

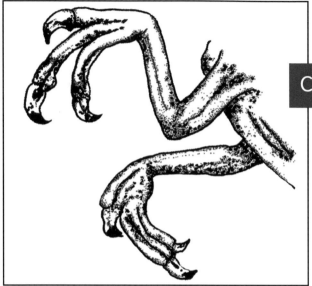

Claws on hands.

Killing claws on feet.

The Velociraptor killed its prey with its claws. The Velociraptor had claws on its hands and feet.

There was a special killing claw on the second toe of each foot. These killing claws were four inches (10 cm) long. They were curved, too.

How did the Velociraptor catch its prey? First, there was the chase. Then, the Velociraptor grabbed its prey with its clawed hands.

WHERE DID THEY LIVE?

The Velociraptors started out in Asia. They followed their prey, the duck-billed dinosaurs, into North America. This move happened about 80 million years ago. This was during the late Cretaceous period.

How did the Velociraptors cross over to North America? They used a land bridge. Then, they spread all over North America.

3 1833 04091 6485

Where the Velociraptor lived in North America.

WHAT WAS THE LAND LIKE?

Ferns, cycads, and palms were growing at that time. These plants are still around today. Also, there were large forests of evergreens, or conifers.

A new kind of plant, angiosperms, began to spread over the land. Angiosperms are plants with flowers and fruit. Cottonwood, beach, sassafras, walnut, and plum trees are angiosperms.

Giant conifers are still around today.

13

THEIR DINOSAUR NEIGHBORS

The Velociraptor lived among many duck-billed dinosaurs. The duck-billed dinosaurs were plant-eaters. They had beaks like parrots. The Maiasaura and the Tenatosaurus were duck-billed dinosaurs.

Maiasaura with its young.

Sauropelta

The Sauropelta was another neighbor of the Velociraptor. It was about 25 feet (8 m) long. The Sauropelta had horny plates all over its back. These plates protected it. The Sauropelta did not like to fight. Like a turtle, the Sauropelta would lie down when it was in danger.

WHO ELSE LIVED THERE?

Small mammals called Multituberculata came to North America about 100 million years ago. We know about over 200 different kinds of Multituberculata.

Some Multituberculata were as small as mice. Others were as big as beavers. The Multituberculata lived for millions of years. Yet, none of them are alive today.

The Ptilodus was a small Multituberculata. It looked like a squirrel and lived in the trees.

A small mammal among Cretaceous plants.

WHAT DID THEY EAT?

A pack of Velociraptors hunting at night.

The Velociraptor was a meat-eater, or carnivore. It hunted for animals. One animal the Velociraptor liked to hunt was the Tenontosaurus.

The Tenontosaurus was as strong and fast as a horse. It could bite with its beak and kick with its back feet. Yet, it could not win a battle with a pack of Velociraptors.

Velociraptors can eat a lot at one time. A pack of 10 Velociraptors could eat a whole Tenontosaurus at one sitting. After this big meal, the Velociraptors would not have to eat again for about 10 days.

The Acrocanthosaurus was an enemy of the Velociraptor. It possibly stole meals from the Velociraptor. This is called scavenging.

The Acrocanthosaurus was a giant dinosaur. It weighed about 5,000 pounds (2,268 kg). It was 40 feet (12 m) long.

The Acrocanthosaurus

This great dinosaur's head was more than four feet (one m) long. It had over 50 sharp teeth. It had strong arms, three-fingered hands, and claws. Big spines covered with skin were on its back.

AMAZING FIND

In 1971, people found a fossil in Mongolia. This fossil showed a Velociraptor and a Protoceratops.

This fossil shows a battle between these two dinosaurs. The Velociraptor had grabbed the Protoceratops's head. This Velociraptor was trying to claw the Protoceraptops. The Protoceratops had the Velociraptor's arm in its beak.

These two dinosaurs continued this battle until a sandstorm came. The sandstorm killed both the Velociraptor and the Protoceraptops.

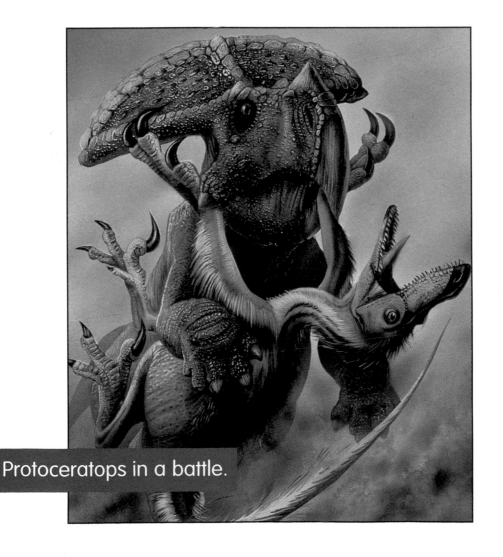

Protoceratops in a battle.

VELOCIRAPTOR FAMILY

Velociraptors lived for more than 50 million years. Paleontologists used to think that all Velociraptors were small animals. They changed their minds when they found a new Velociraptor fossil.

This new fossil showed a very big Velociraptor. It was about 20 feet (6 m) long. It may have weighed up to 2,000 pounds (907 kg). They named this new kind of Velociraptor. They called it Utahraptor.

The Utahraptor had a lot in common with the Velociraptor. Both had large brains, good eyesight, strong legs, and killing claws. The Utahraptor's killing claw was bigger.

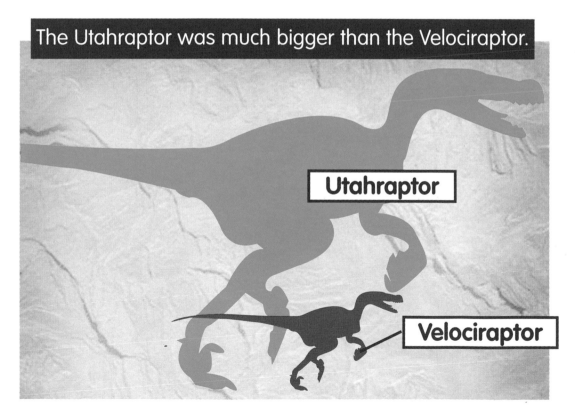

The Utahraptor was much bigger than the Velociraptor.

Utahraptor

Velociraptor

DISCOVERY

In July, 1923, many Americans went to the Flaming Cliffs Formation of the Gobi Desert. This is in southern Mongolia. They were looking for fossils.

These Americans uncovered many fossils. They found fossils of the Oviraptor, the Saurornithoides, and the Velociraptor. This was the first time someone found a Velociraptor fossil.

This Velociraptor fossil was not complete. They only found the head, a finger, a few claws, and part of a foot. In 1924, H. F. Osborn named the Velociraptor.

Velociraptor skull

WHERE ARE THEY TODAY?

American Museum of Natural History
Central Park West at 79th Street
New York, NY 10024
www.amnh.org

Museum of Comparative Zoology
Harvard University
26 Oxford St
Cambridge, MA 02138
www.mcz.harvard.edu

Peabody Museum of Natural History
Yale University
P.O. Box 208118
170 Whitney Avenue
New Haven, CT 06520-8118
www.peabody.yale.edu

VELOCIRAPTOR

NAME MEANS	Speedy Burglar
DIET	Meat
LENGTH	6 feet (2 m)
HEIGHT	3 feet (1 m)
TIME	Late Cretaceous Period
FAMILY	Theropod
SPECIAL FEATURE	Killing claws
FOSSILS FOUND	USA—Maryland, Montana Oklahoma, Wyoming Elsewhere—Mongolia, China, Korea, Russia, Canada

Velociraptor lived 80 million years ago

First humans appeared 1.6 million years ago

Triassic Period	Jurassic Period	Cretaceous Period	Tertiary Period
245 Million years ago	208 Million years ago	144 Million years ago	65 Million years ago
Mesozoic Era			Cenozoic Era

FUN DINOSAUR WEB SITES

Zoom Dinosaurs
www.EnchantedLearning.com/subjects/dinosaurs
Zoom Dinosaurs, designed for students of all ages, includes an illustrated dinosaur dictionary and classroom activities.

Dinosaur Illustrations
www.search4dinosaurs.com/pictures.html
This invaluable site features numerous illustrations of dinosaurs and other prehistoric animals.

Dino Russ's Lair
www.isgs.uiuc.edu/dinos/dinos_home.html
This informative site features information on a variety of dinosaurs, as well as dinosaur eggs, dinosaur exhibits, dinosaur digs, and other prehistoric vertebrates.

IMPORTANT WORDS

angiosperm plants and trees with flowers and fruit.

carnivore a meat-eater.

conifers trees that have needles instead of leaves. Conifers stay green all year long.

Cretaceous period period of time that happened 144-65 million years ago.

cycads palmlike plants or trees.

dinosaur reptiles that lived on land 248–65 million years ago.

fossil remains of very old animals and plants. People commonly find fossils in the ground.

land bridge a small piece of land that binds two larger land areas.

mammal warm-blooded animals that feed milk to their young.

paleontologist someone who studies very old life (like dinosaurs), mostly by studying fossils.

prey the animals that are hunted for food.

scavenger animals that eat dead animals that they did not kill themselves.

INDEX